ADDICTED TO MISERY

The Other Side Of Co-dependency

Robert A. Becker, Ph.D.

Health Communications, Inc.
Deerfield Beach, Florida

Robert A. Becker
St. Louis, Missouri

Library of Congress Cataloging-in-Publication Data

Becker, Robert A., 1948-
  Addicted to misery: the other side of co-dependency/by
Robert A. Becker.
      p.   cm.
    ISBN 1-55874-029-5
    1. Co-dependence (Psychology)   I. Title
RC569.5.C63B44   1989   89-1874
616.86—dc19   CIP

©1989 Robert A. Becker
ISBN 1-55874-029-5

Published by: Health Communications, Inc.
                  Enterprise Center
                  3201 S.W. 15th Street
                  Deerfield Beach, Florida 33442

Cover design by Reta Thomas

DEDICATION

To my wife, Deborah

ACKNOWLEDGMENTS

Many people helped in the writing of this book. The inspiration for the ideas which form its basic concept came from my patients; from them, too, a sharper insight into myself.

I thank Rokelle Lerner, who introduced me to Gary Seidler of Health Communications, Inc. From the start, Gary's understanding of the concept of the book and his ongoing support sustained my own commitment.

I appreciate the encouragement of my sons, Jason and David, who were always interested in the book's progress. My stepsons, Robert, Patrick, Matthew and Gary, ages 4 to 8, were enthusiastic about the project, though I suspect their interest was, at times, in knowing exactly when they might reclaim the family computer and put it to better use.

Finally, I am grateful to my wife, Deborah. As my resident editor, proofreader, one-woman think tank and cheering section, Deborah's skilled and loving support enabled me to complete the book at a time when we were also planning our wedding, blending our two families and dealing with a host of work-related problems. She passed the ultimate test when I told her I would have to finish writing the manuscript during our honeymoon. Her comment: "I'll just have to find something else to do with my time."

CONTENTS

INTRODUCTION

For years, I have worked with co-dependents and adult children of alcoholics. Many were recovering chemical dependents themselves or living in dependent relationships. The most striking phenomenon I saw was those people who, after working hard to alleviate many life stresses or at least to regain some manageability in their lives, then returned to the state of misery they were in before coming to therapy. Time and time again, they attained a level of successful emotional functioning, working through the obstacles and conflicts and then, with full awareness, they would march right back to unhappiness and emotional distress.

As with most co-dependents and adult children of alcoholics, they had family histories of dysfunctional characteristics ranging from moderate to severe. Verbal, emotional and physical abuse was common. Yet the clearest marks left by their past characterized them as people generally incapable of perceiving themselves in adequate, approving or worthwhile ways. Their level of emotional openness and the ability to identify their pain barely existed. Oftentimes, when I simply asked, "What hurts?" they could only say, "I don't know, I only know I hurt." It would take several sessions to get them to a point where they could identify the specifics of the hurts in their lives.

The work done in the area of treating co-dependency initially helped me and certainly explained many of the behaviors I saw in them. It made sense that if as children their feelings were internalized as a result of oppressive and repressive emotional environments, their openness and emotional expression as adults would be poor and their ability to be specific about their feelings would be extremely limited. With the exception of anger, most feelings were never shared or processed. These children became adults without the skills to trust, feel, or talk — all characteristics of co-dependency.

Focusing on the specific co-dependency issues in therapy had good results at first. Accepting who they were and the realities associated with this put them into a positive stage for recovery. The acceptance they began to feel by attending self-help groups like Adult Children of Alcoholics (ACoA) furthered their improvement. Some even started making peace with themselves. They began to express and identify feelings, something previously not possible. The co-dependent ways stopped and real self-satisfaction began.

However, in spite of these successes and often feeling good, they developed an obsession with some catastrophic expectation regarding how to maintain their new success or their fear of what the changes might bring. Behaviorally, you could see their progress and movement away from the misery with which they entered therapy, only to be drawn back to it when their catastrophic expectations emerged. Where did the catastrophic expectations come from? Detailed family-of-origin work with them pointed to traumas they experienced as children living with constant stress. As adults, those painful memories reappeared to set the stage emotionally for the development of the catastrophic expectations so commonly observed.

Regardless of what discomfort they came to therapy with, it seemed that some psychological phenomenon allowed them to disavow their painful reality and return to the misery they so desperately wished to leave. This happened to people who were doing well and enjoying their new freedom. More than any others, my co-dependent clients and adult children of alcoholics were the most vulnerable to the catastrophic scenario. They elevated anxiety and fear levels significantly as a result of the catastrophic expectations they had about their new situations. Letting go of their rescuing and caretaking styles and moving toward acknowledging their need for self-acceptance and celebration were the hardest to do. They created great hypothetical monsters to prevent further growth and recovery from co-dependency and adult child issues or they began to dismantle their new thinking and belief systems, reverting to the old ones.

Worse, the unfamiliarity with their recovering attitudes and situations seemed pivotal to the development of expectations which had no rational basis. The familiarity with catastrophic trauma as children spawned these new expectations of doom and gloom. Often, they would marvel at the relief they felt, saying, "I'm feeling great this week . . . but it won't last."

Even more destructive to their recovery was any event or situation which went, as life frequently does, in a negative direction. Their approach to this was, "I'm having a terrible week . . . but I expected this." Breaking this well-reinforced thinking pattern was perverse. Having to get rid of the irrational expectations made the task more complicated. Yet unless I could assist them in seeing how their thinking precluded any lasting happiness, it was clear they would restore themselves to misery.

Getting better depended upon their insight and willingness to change. First, the catastrophic scenario had to be recognized, going back and breaking through the denial — "My family life was fine. Those bad things didn't happen." Piecing that together and seeing how they had made the bridge to catastrophic expectations was next. Then, the thinking associated with this had to be modified from, "I can't make it with these changes," to "It may be frightening for a while but I will survive. I will make it."

Once I was able to help them develop emotional sanctuaries while they lived through the changes, the co-dependent thinking and beliefs broke down.

The final step was to become comfortable with their recovery and end the addiction to misery. This meant getting used to feeling good, having things go right, enjoying themselves and coping with life, until recovery became as familiar as misery once was.

This book takes you through the steps to identify if and how you are addicted to misery. It points out how overtly the addiction seems like just bad luck. Most important, it helps you to recognize what catastrophic scenarios you have developed and how to overcome them. Finally, it gives specific ways to leave the misery behind and begin to enjoy happiness, without waiting for the ax to fall.

Many of the chapters end with a section entitled "Laboratory Experiments." When I was in high school, I remember trying some dangerous things in my chemistry lab. However, as good old Mr. Young would tell us budding scientists, "This is a controlled environment. Nothing can go wrong here." He was right. No matter how many explosions we had, only that room caught fire. In this book, the *Laboratory Experiments* are designed to have you try things on paper and in your head. These are safe places where you will not create any real problems but where you can experiment with new ideas and thoughts.

ONE

Co-dependency — The Word Of The Decade

What Is Co-dependency?

The notion of co-dependency is relatively new. It has certainly become a word with significance and master status identification in the 1980s. Many books, articles and programs have appeared giving attention to those people who either grew up in alcoholic families or are living with dependent people.

Other than some people involved in the chemical dependency field, this concept only recently came into the public spotlight. My first encounter with the term "co-dependency" was at a conference on alcoholism and drug addiction. The presenter was describing a phenomenon that each of us working in the field would fall prey to. In fact, he insisted that we had all become "co-dependents," that is, we had taken on many of the characteristics of the patients we worked with, without the chemical effects of drugs or alcohol. I remember he asked us to describe how much

1

more "managing" we had become since working in the treatment center. How significant had issues of power and control become for us in dealing with such power- and control-oriented patients? He made it clear that the disease's dynamics would interact with our basic need, as helping professionals, to rescue and fix our patients. He warned us that our own power struggles would ultimately render us powerless and those characteristics we brought to the treatment center, the "unfinished business" in our personal lives, would determine the level of co-dependent characteristics we would exhibit.

The term co-dependency still seemed vague. The only parts of the concept that had relevance dealt with power and control issues and the notion of being a rescuer. Later I began reading and attending workshops specifically on co-dependency, the alcoholic family and dysfunctional families and relationships. The curious thing was, I had been seeing most of the characteristics of co-dependency in my private practice and in myself for years yet never had put a label on our dysfunctional behavior. We all felt inadequate and disapproved of and found little satisfaction in life, regardless of our accomplishments.

I remember a client who was referred to me through his company's Employee Assistance Program, with complaints of depression. He was a middle-aged man, a third-line manager with a Fortune 500 company. He earned a magnificent salary, had generous employee benefits, was well respected in the company and in line for a regional vice-president's job within six months. He described his family as loving and warm. He was also a partner in a very successful high-tech company.

As I proceeded with my clinical interview, I was able to rule out depressive illness. However, as we talked, he described his experiences growing up in an alcoholic family. As a boy, he never felt adequate at anything. He never received any approval, in spite of getting straight As in school. As he moved into adulthood and graduated from college, he began his career with the company. He moved through the corporate ranks vigorously, although he never once derived any pleasure from his accomplishments. On several occasions, in fact, he found himself purposely sabotaging his own successes. He concluded that his lack of satisfaction was due to his depression. I pointed out how little, if at all, his childhood experience had prepared him for self-enjoyment or acknowledgment, and I suggested that he was probably incapable of any self-pleasure or recognition. He felt miserable and nothing in life provided satisfaction.

When comparing this man's symptoms of co-dependency with the writings in the field, he fit almost any definition.

Robert Subby, director of Family Systems, Inc., in Minneapolis, defines co-dependency in the book, *Lost In The Shuffle*, as:

> ". . . An emotional, psychological, and behavioral condition that develops as a result of an individual's prolonged exposure to, and practice of, a set of oppressive rules — rules which prevent the open expression of feeling, as well as the direct discussion of personal and interpersonal problems."

Melody Beattie, in *Co-Dependent No More*, describes a co-dependent as:

> ". . . A person who has let someone else's behavior affect him or her and is obsessed with controlling other people's behavior."

Definitions are plentiful but the place to start assessing co-dependency must be its symptoms. The following is a list of symptoms of co-dependency presented by many professionals. I should note that my clients and I have exhibited most of them.

Symptoms Of Co-dependency

1. Forced as a child to hurry up and grow up, that is, to take on significant adult responsibilities. "I had to make sure my brothers and sisters got to school because Mom was sick most mornings."

2. Developed very rigid attitudes early in life. Result: doesn't ask to have needs met. "I don't need anybody's help. I can handle it alone."

3. Has extreme difficulty being emotionally expressive. "I don't talk about my feelings — that's nobody's business."

4. Has difficulty establishing close interpersonal relationships. Has little trust in others. "I don't let anyone get too close. I would only get hurt."

5. Feels nervous, often on mental alert. "I find it is hard to relax, even when I'm exhausted."

6. Has exaggerated need for approval from others. "I just want to make everyone happy, just to please them."

7. Represses memory — tells himself the bad things he experienced growing up didn't happen. "I didn't have it so bad at home. I know many kids who had it a lot worse."

8. Attempts to convince himself that he would be happy, if only *(someone else)* would change. "When I make my mother happy, I'll quit feeling guilty."

9. Lives life as a chronic victim and is extremely serious. Does not know how to experience happiness. "I can't believe the way things always turn against me, but that's how life is for me."

10. Has difficulty experiencing *normal* feelings. "I feel unhappy most of the time but when I don't, it feels strange and I never expect the happiness to last."

11. Feels high level of anxiety in day-to-day situations. "I'm okay with changes as long as they are very specific [black and white]. But, it makes me very nervous when I can't predict the outcome [gray]."

12. Has extreme fear of abandonment. "I know it's crazy to live with him, but I could never make it without him."

Co-dependency And Addiction

Co-dependents find themselves in unenviable relationships with addicts of all types. Regardless of the addiction, those living with addicts are affected by their behavior.

The temptation to change the addict is all but irresistible. Scheming, plotting and planning ways to control the dependent person becomes the obsession of almost everyone living with an addict. This is where co-dependency grows and emerges as a lifestyle. This battle for control and power becomes the main cause of dependent relationships and defines how each person will function.

Co-dependents assume the role of rescuer and fixer, to help the dependent person and stop their own misery. Dependent persons assume the role of victim and scapegoat and look for ways to maintain and rationalize their addiction.

The co-dependent's relationship with an addicted person becomes an important one in that the two create a very enmeshed partnership, supporting one another's needs. This support system becomes the fabric which weaves the two together in a life of endless misery.

The significance with which these relationships grew and evolved fostered the concept of Adult Children of Alcoholics. The problems brought on by these relationships could no longer be ignored and so "Adult Children" was born.

"Adult Children"

The term *Adult Children* has recently been coined and refers to people who grew up in alcoholic families. Much has been written about adult children of alcoholics. Claudia Black, in her book, *It Will Never Happen To Me*, defined three basic rules that such children lived with: *don't talk; don't trust;* and, *don't feel.* If you grew up in a fairly average alcoholic family, you can certainly relate to these rules.

You didn't *talk* because everybody was too busy with the chaos created by the alcoholic parent. Besides, who had the time to listen? You didn't *trust!* Early in life you learned that parents often did not mean what they said or say what they meant. You did not trust your role models. In fact, it could be assumed that all grown-ups were untrustworthy; you couldn't trust anyone. Finally, growing up in an alcoholic family certainly taught you not to *feel*. The alcoholic family didn't tolerate feelings, especially the bad ones. Suppressing and keeping your feelings inside was the way you handled your feelings.

These conditions, which shaped so much of the personality of the child in an alcoholic family, are not unique to alcoholic families. The same rules applied in divorced families; families with significant medical or psychological illness; families where the parents were not themselves alcoholic but grew up in alcoholic families, passing the traits on to their children; families where parents were absent; or any family with other significant dysfunction.

Adult children are those who grew up in virtually any dysfunctional environment, fertile ground for the development of another addiction — *addiction to misery*. Familiarity with unhappiness, stress and misery created by the dysfunctional home produced perfect recruits for becoming addicted to misery.

The study of adult children in this country has identified the profound effect that *who, where,* and *how* we grew up explains much of our adult behavior, beliefs and attitudes. The point is that adult children of alcoholics don't have the market cornered on misery and co-dependency. Many more of us who struggled in some type of dysfunctional family also suffered and the resounding conclusion was that familiarity with unhappiness and misery; poor self-esteem; repression of feelings; over-worrying or over-anticipating; the need to please, rescue or fix became our mainstay. The groundwork was laid for our addiction to misery.

<u>Laboratory Experiments</u>

1. Look at the *Symptoms of Co-dependency* section. Write down the way you see yourself with regard to each symptom. Try to remember when the symptom began and what was going on at that time in your life. Now, rate your level of each symptom from 1 (low) to 5 (high). Add the scores and note your level of co-dependency.

     0-12 Occasionally affected by others but not generally a problem.

     13-24 Probable co-dependent characteristics. Certainly time to look at how others affect you and your feelings.

     25-36 Co-dependent characteristics. Scoring in this range suggests you should evaluate what you do when experiencing these symptoms.

     37+ Seriously co-dependent. Seek professional help to develop a plan to stop the pain from these symptoms.

2. Think of ways in which you might try to change. Write down these ideas for later reference.

TWO

Addictions

The word *addiction* appears in Webster's dictionary as:

> n. condition of being a slave to a habit; strong inclination, devotion to a habit.

This total, consuming dependency on something, without regard for consequences, is what makes the notion of addiction so incredible.

Alcohol-dependent or addicted persons (alcoholics), commonly sacrifice jobs and families in order not to address their addiction and quit drinking. Yet when asked, they place the highest value on having a good job and family life.

People who are drug-addicted often engage in illegal activities just to get their drugs. This sociopathic behavior may be extremely foreign to them yet the need for their dependency preempts any and all concern for society's rules. The risk of arrest, embarrassment, conviction and prison all seem a reasonable price to satisfy their addictive needs.

Eating disorders or addictions fall into three categories. Anorexics are those persons who starve themselves, put their bodies at high risk for a multitude of symptoms which could result in heart failure and death, although, when asked if they want to die, they generally deny it. Bulimics, those who binge on enormous amounts of food (10,000 calories and more), then induce vomiting, many times rival the financial problems of drug addicts because of what appears to be an insatiable need for food. Obese persons, too, risk serious medical complications and social rejection even though most obese people wish to be accepted and liked.

Gambling and sexual addicts suffer severe consequences for their behavior and addictions. Gamblers face financial ruin for themselves and for anyone who backs them. Sex addicts risk harsh legal and societal consequences for their behavior but they seem ready to do so in order to satisfy their needs.

Addiction To Misery

Persons *addicted to misery* (ATMs) are chronically miserable or anticipating the return of a miserable state. Two conditions prevail for ATMs. First, they remain in their misery because of the catastrophic expectations they create surrounding those changes needed to stop being miserable. An example of this might be, "Living with my husband may be terrible, but I don't think I could make it without his money," or "I hate this job; it makes me miserable but I couldn't find another job anywhere and we might lose our home."

Second, if they find their way out of the miserable state or condition, then happiness, self-satisfaction and pleasure are so foreign to them that the unfamiliarity acts to sabotage the relief they feel. The classic example of this is, "I love the way things are going but I know it can't last." Or "I've never been so happy or felt so free but something is going to go wrong."

Psychologically, when we expect something so much, we either go out and look for it or it inevitably finds us. In either case, we return to the misery.

A working definition of persons who are *addicted to misery* is:

> **Persons who have experienced a chronic and prolonged state of misery or unhappiness and maintained that misery by creating catastrophic expectations about the changes required to stop the addiction; and/ or who, once the changes occur, experience significant discomfort with happiness, self-satisfaction and pleasure, such that they cause either purposeful or directed behaviors to return them to the misery.**

Going back to the concept of how powerful and consuming addictions are is the basis for understanding how they work. When we see people prepared to give up someone warm and caring who will kiss them goodnight in exchange for some white powder; or trade a good job for the bottle; or look into a mirror at an emaciated body and say, "Look at that bulge where my skin is overlapping;" or steal every penny they can to play the horses — we begin to understand the power and control that addictions have. Addictions maintain totally inappropriate behaviors without regard for any consequences.

Elements Of All Addictions

All addictions, whether to alcohol, drugs, food, sex, co-dependency, misery or whatever, have six main components: 1) denial; 2) loss of control, or powerlessness; 3) continued usage without regard for consequences; 4) repression of feelings; 5) obsessive-compulsive thoughts and behavior; 6) withdrawal symptoms.

Denial

Addictions of all types begin with denial. Recognizing and admitting that which creates problems in his life is the last thing an addict wants to do. Disavowing painful reality is a very normal thing for us to do, especially if recognizing our problem means we must make hard decisions which could affect the basic structure of our lives.

Admitting that we are helplessly caught in a relationship with an addicted spouse or friend, being attached to that person and finding our every move directed by the addiction, is painful and frightening. Looking honestly into ourselves and seeing that we are prepared to trade our loved ones or an excellent job for the bottle or drug is oftentimes impossible. So often we say, "I've already fouled things up, so it's easier to let it go on than face more shame and embarrassment."

Denial of our addiction provides us two possibilities. One is to avoid making changes which might result in further failure. The second is to avoid rejection by others which might occur even if we made the necessary changes. These two forces alone keep the denial going.

Loss Of Control — Powerlessness

By the nature of addiction, the loss of control or powerlessness, is at the center of all addiction symptoms. The alcoholic or drug-addicted person is unable to "use" socially without the loss of control. It is not possible to predict the outcome of any usage. This pervasive condition makes life unmanageable and before too long, serious consequences result.

You see this phenomenon in eating-disordered, sexually-addicted, gambling-addicted, chemically-dependent, and co-dependent persons, clear examples of loss of control resulting from addiction; a sense of total powerlessness exists. Anorexic, bulimic and obese persons all use food in a manner such that they clearly seem to be powerless over its effect. The food itself seems to trigger uncontrollable behaviors that result in unmanageable consumption and life situations. Sex addicts and gamblers find themselves in the same loss-of-control and powerless states. Co-dependents lose emotional control in their attempt to control others. The controlling of others becomes the main element that takes away the control and makes life unmanageable for the co-dependent, as alcohol does to an alcoholic.

Continued Usage Without Regard For Consequences

All addictions have this feature. It doesn't matter what consequences the addict faces due to continued usage, the only thing that matters is to follow the needs of the addiction. Loss of job, family, threat of imprisonment, financial ruin, physical danger have little or no meaning when the addiction's needs call out. I've seen people opt to go to jail because they thought they could get drugs more easily there. Others give up their husbands, wives and children in order not to make changes and deal with their dependencies. Co-dependents remain in emotionally and physically abusive marriages for years just to avoid changing themselves and addressing their co-dependent ways. The idea that it doesn't matter is so powerful that even the addicts cannot believe the actions of their co-dependents.

Repression Of Feelings

To repress one's feelings is like over-stuffing garbage in a trash bag. Eventually, it becomes so full that it explodes, throwing its contents everywhere. Now you've got garbage all over and no one wants to come near it. The same thing happens with feelings. After stuffing so long, you usually end up exploding and everybody wants to get away and stay away. Repressing or pushing feelings down and not letting them come out is common for all addicts.

People who become addicted to misery are excellent repressors of feelings. By doing so, they are able to pretend they don't feel, and they don't have to act upon those feelings. But once someone cares enough about themselves, they must deal with and accept their feelings.

Obsessive-Compulsive Thoughts And Behavior

Addictions of all types are characterized by obsessive or constant thoughts having to do with some aspect of controlling the addiction. Planning and scheming when, where and how to "use" is common for alcoholic and drug-dependent persons. Co-dependents constantly let the behavior of others affect them, then become obsessed with thinking of ways to control the others.

Compulsive behavior is seen in the almost untiring efforts the addict makes to satisfy his or her addictions. A woman once told me of an incredibly intricate scheme she devised to obtain "speed" (amphetamines), her drug of choice. She told of waiting in the lobbies of medical buildings and approaching obese women there. She offered to trade them Valiums, which she obtained from various doctors, in return for diet pills. She knew that most doctors would not turn down an obese woman requesting such a drug. In a matter of three months, she built a network of fifteen doctors whom she and six obese women visited monthly to obtain drugs for trading. When I heard the story, I couldn't believe the lengths to which she would go. This pointed to the obsessive-compulsive element of her addiction.

One co-dependent woman who constantly blamed all her unhappiness on an alcoholic husband, devised one plan after another to get him to stop drinking. When he finally entered treatment and began recovery, she found their relationship so unexciting that she returned to her obsessional thinking in an attempt to get him to return to drinking.

Withdrawal Symptoms

Whatever your addiction — alcohol, drugs, food, sex, gambling or people — when you stop the addiction, some kind of withdrawal occurs. Alcoholics and drug addicts might experience physical symptoms like blood pressure changes or the shakes. When leaving an abusive relationship, you become nervous, anxious and hypervigilant (having an obsessive need to be on guard).

The typical withdrawal symptom for misery addicts is discomfort with the unfamiliarity of misery's absence. This withdrawal, which keeps us hooked on unhappiness, is a key element as we will discuss in later chapters.

The First Step

At the heart of all anonymous self-help groups is the basic Step 1:

"We have admitted we were powerless over (the addiction) and that our lives have become unmanageable."

Understanding what you must accept in order to begin recovery from any addiction is fundamental to this First Step notion. The part of powerlessness that makes acceptance so hard is seeing oneself as "less than" or "not as good as" others. Remember, addicts are already feeling significantly inadequate. Having to admit to being "powerless" magnifies the enormity of their feelings of worthlessness and their poor self-concept.

Medicators Of Life

When I visit the dentist and he tells me he is going to pull a tooth, I ask for all the medication I need to kill the pain. The same thing is true in life in dealing with emotional pain. Somehow, all humans have the ability to disavow painful reality, that is, to deny what they don't want to deal with. Loneliness, boredom, fear, hurt, sadness, rejection, painful feelings are things we always want to ignore or avoid. That is human nature and we have learned that we can use other things to medicate those feelings, just like the anesthetics the dentist uses to prevent pain.

I've never met an addicted person who invented a new emotion; but the addiction, to alcohol, drugs, food, sex, gambling or whatever, acted as a medicator, allowing the addict to disavow the painful reality he felt, providing a very powerful reinforcer and emotional bond to the addiction. Let's face it, if drinking temporarily removes the feeling of loneliness; if drugging stops the pain of rejection; if eating satisfies the void of boredom, doesn't it make sense that the medicating effects will keep the addiction going? Anything that feels better than stopping and changing will maintain the addiction for years, through drastic consequences, before some change occurs.

In the course of prolonged exposure, we become familiar with the scenario and our misery grows as change continues to be avoided. This is very important in misery addiction.

Laboratory Experiments

1. Look at *Elements of All Addictions*. Determine how these things may apply to your present life. See if you can relate what you do to maintain these elements.
2. Define what medicators you use and write out some situations describing this. Evaluate how effective the medicators you use are in helping your situation and your feelings.
3. Think about the changes you might consider making to feel better. Write them down.
4. Develop a list of the things you worry about most. Break this down into daily, weekly and monthly worries.

THREE

Getting Familiar
With Misery

Co-dependency teaches us many ways of dealing with life. Unfortunately, these ways often create prolonged unhappiness, making us so familiar with misery that we come to feel it is normal. We learn that being unhappy and having things go wrong is to be expected. Whether our co-dependency expectations come from the families we grew up in or from living with someone who is dependent, we are prepared for a life with many disappointments, frustrations and misery. Getting used to the traumas and unpredictable situations is hard at first, but we do learn, in order to survive. These experiences shape our thinking such that we imagine and experience situation after situation that is never what we want, never the way it should be, never right. This is where our familiarity with misery begins as a co-dependent.

Pre-existing Developmental Impairments

Children growing up in dysfunctional (another new word) families where things are out of control, develop emotional impairments which stay with them for life. These may take the form of not trusting themselves or others, inability to talk about their feelings, and the most hurtful, the inability to feel their feelings. Imagine the frustration of having something that hurts inside your body, yet not being able to point to where the pain is. Additionally, we become rigid and inflexible, we only like things that are either black or white, right or wrong, and we hate situations that leave unclear results. When that happens, we have feelings of nervousness and anxiety that we can't explain but we suffer with them patiently. As adults we see the world this way and cope with it by seeking ways to deal with our distrust, repression of feelings and rigidity. Avoiding boredom, finding excitement and looking for approval and acceptance become our daily tasks.

These conditions set the emotional stage for us to develop co-dependency. They also dictate the direction that many of our adult interpersonal relationships will take. Tragically, we choose persons to have relationships with for all the wrong reasons — reasons like: "He needs me. I can make him better. Who will take care of him if I don't? I know I can make him happier than he has ever been. I don't think I can get anybody else." These reasons show how we feel about ourselves. Woody Allen had a line in his movie, *Annie Hall*, that fits co-dependents so well. "I would never want to be a member of a club that would have me as a member."

Who would really take us seriously? Our only real value lies in what we can do for others and that is never appreciated. Our self-image is so poor, our way of addressing feelings so inadequate, that we remain hopelessly stuck. We need to understand the origins of these conditions if any meaningful change is to occur in our lives.

Internalizing Feelings And Our Self-Image

Probably the earliest behavior we learn in getting familiar with misery is to internalize or stuff our feelings. Simply put, this means we don't talk about what feels bad, what feels good, what feels sad or what we feel. Instead, we keep the feelings inside and try to make them go away. Having to push our emotions inside makes us feel that no one cares. For a child, this is devastating. Unresponsive parents, caught up in their own problems, give children inaccurate messages. The distressed mother, struggling with her alcoholic husband, is oftentimes too preoccupied to deal with the emotional needs of her child. I've seen this over and over with many adult children of alcoholics. They say, "I never talked about how I felt. I was too busy trying to help keep the peace. I never felt anyone cared."

David's story shows perfectly how this works. David was a 44-year-old married man who came to me complaining of depression and a general dissatisfaction with both his professional and his personal life. After some time, it became evident that David had never been or felt satisfied with any of his successes or accomplishments. As we discussed his growing up, he talked about his alcoholic father, who constantly belittled and criticized him. In spite of his excellent grades in school and his achievements in sports, his father made it clear that he was never good enough. His was a good alcoholic family and feelings, especially bad ones, were rarely tolerated. He learned early in life to keep his feelings to himself. That way, no one could hurt him or use them against him. This process of internalizing feelings was important in surviving the pain of living in an alcoholic family. Even as a small boy, he knew that crying enraged his father and would result in greater emotional and physical pain. His mother seldom showed any feelings except anger. This further reinforced the behavior of doing nothing with his feelings except to stuff them deep inside, hoping they would go away.

His self-image never had a chance to develop positively. Most of the time, he wondered what he had done wrong and why his dad never liked him. As he grew, he developed little self-confidence, shied away from people, became dependent upon his own independence for everything, trusted nobody and lived miserably from day to day.

Familiar Versus Unfamiliar Experiences

For David his experiences as a boy had very negative consequences. He was taught to stuff feelings, distrust his own judgement, and in general, to feel he was not worth a damn. The early experience he was most familiar with was painful. As he explained, he came to expect that "Most things will go wrong." Any pleasure he derived from his accomplishments was quickly erased and he rarely expected things to go right for long. His expectations were negative and pessimistic. Familiarity with happiness was nonexistent.

Power And Control

The experiences of a child living in a dysfunctional home, be it alcoholic, abusive, divorced or emotionally dead, certainly teach two things — first, how important it is to gain as much control in life as possible, and second, never to be powerless over anything because being powerless means to lack control and having no control results in misery.

Dysfunctional families give us the terrible feeling of being out of control and the knowledge of how powerless we are. You make a pact with yourself early in life that, as soon as possible, you will gain control and have power over the events of your life. You can see this happen in young children when they begin withdrawing from people. They shy away from others, especially grown-ups, and want to be left alone. This is the root of shyness or self-centered fear of what others might think about us. Yet we do this as a way to use our power to stop others from controlling us.

Dependent On Feeling Miserable

As the emotional trauma of our dysfunctional family unfolds, teaching us so many wrong realities, our co-dependency is spawned. Seeing the world as chaotic, out of control and not meaningful, forces us to learn to cope in poor ways. Yet, living with constant stress causes us to use defenses to deal with the real world. We become defended rather than defensive. The psychic numbing, or repression of memory and feelings, starts the misery which begins the dependency. It is what we come to expect. It is what feels normal. It is what we miss when it is absent. We depend on feeling miserable and we find the uncertainty, when that misery subsides, to be frustrating, worrisome and downright uncomfortable.

Attachment And Detachment

Getting familiar with misery teaches us many painful things. The relationships we form become places of great misery, making loneliness and disassociation the only sanctuary for an absence of misery.

Attachment is a process whereby you become emotionally and physically dependent on someone to take care of you. Children attach to parents as a means of survival. The process is appropriate in that case but when adults attach themselves to other adults, relationships are threatened, power and control issues are great and sick dependencies are spawned.

Even though closeness is avoided, misery addicts and co-dependents often become attached to people and relationships that are destructive, uncaring and unsupportive. The attachment provides a false sense of security and belonging. For most ATMs and co-dependents, fear of abandonment is so great that they will do anything to avoid it. This comes from living in families where people were never really there for them emotionally.

The main problem with attachment is the pain and restriction of freedom experienced by being so emotionally connected to someone. The dependency on this attachment makes it impossible to be independent and secure. Until the co-dependent learns to detach, recovery is threatened.

Detachment is a process of letting go of that "I can't live without this person" feeling. To detach, self-confidence must emerge and the person's self-reliance must take over. When I explain this to my clients, sometimes they think I am suggesting that they stop loving or caring about their spouses or partners. As I discussed earlier, *taking care of* is a very unhealthy process, though *caring for* is certainly desirable. Detaching is learning to care for, not take care of. It is a process of becoming un-dependent on the effects of others. This prevents us from being controlled by the emotional needs of others, or worse, trying to change them, as a way to feel better.

Anhedonia

Most of the discussion in this chapter has been to explain the process of how we get familiar with misery. It is important to understand this and see what getting familiar with misery does to us emotionally.

Anhedonia is a psychological condition, defined as *the inability to be happy, have fun, or experience common sensual pleasures.* Becoming familiar with misery results in just these things. We don't consider ourselves emotionally ill but we find it difficult to balance unpleasant experiences with pleasant ones. As experiences accumulate and we are chronically unhappy and scared, we become anhedonic. Another way to view anhedonia is as a state of numbness. So often, as people seek help, they discover how difficult it is to identify any feelings, after such prolonged exposure to these conditions.

This inability to be happy is not symptomatic only of depression. Certainly, a symptom of depression is the loss of interest in common activities, but that disappears after successful intervention with medication or psychotherapy. This symptom, loss of pleasure, remains only until the biochemical elements kick in, in an endogenous depression caused by a chemical imbalance in the brain. In a reactive depression there is a direct causal connection to a situation, e.g. in a divorce, once the person has therapeutically worked through the trauma or crisis, he is able to revert to normal functioning and experience pleasure once again.

Not so with ATMs! ATMs who have left the reactive situations which caused loss of pleasure may continue to have the symptom for up to two years. Their anhedonia is connected to their long familiar history of misery and even when life improves, things just don't feel good.

This condition must be identified and worked with as a treatment issue if the addiction to misery is to be dismantled. Due to chronic unhappy experiences, it will take time for the emotional system to respond to things as they really are. During the recovery period, we will have to work very hard at identifying and processing these good feelings until they are familiar.

Laboratory Experiments

1. Try to remember what the rules were in your home when you were growing up. Identify what your family taught you about your feelings, about trusting and talking. Be specific.
2. If stuffing feelings is what you generally do, think back to when this began. Ask yourself why? Work hard at remembering how feelings were dealt with while you were growing up. List specific situations when you remember not being able to express feelings.
3. Explore what you think was familiar for you as a child about trusting others, risking, caring for yourself.
4. Think about how long you have felt miserable and how many times, when things were going well, you somehow found a way to mess them up and get back to the misery.

FOUR

Worry: The Catalyst Of Misery

It should be clear now how significant our early experiences are in developing the image we have of ourselves. If, as children, we received praise and encouragement from our parents, this contributed to our early development of good self-concept. Seeing our parents show concern for us and others taught us sensitivity. Watching as they entered into risking situations showed us how to trust. Seeing them share their feelings with one another in caring and compassionate ways educated us in ways to express feelings.

However, if our family repressed feelings, criticized and didn't show caring, and taught us that we couldn't trust anyone, then we began our journey into adulthood with pre-existing impairments for interacting with people and having relationships. Further, a child who rarely feels accomplishment is never comfortable accepting praise or compliments as an adult. What basis would there be to believe them?

When we discussed pre-existing developmental impairments in the last chapter, we began to see the foundation being laid for our familiarity with misery. We also observed how this familiarity with unhappiness versus happiness prepared us to expect things to go wrong and to expect the worst. It is this locking into misery that starts the cycle of addiction to misery.

Locking Into Misery

Locking into, or getting hooked on the present miserable or uncomfortable situation is not as hard as it sounds. When someone living in an abusive relationship asks for help, tell them, "Just get out! Leave. Throw the abuser out!"

I didn't need eight years of advanced education, two years of internship, state licensing and a million dollars in malpractice insurance to know that. It is simple. If it hurts, remove the thing that is causing the hurt. Although this makes sense, it rarely worked for my clients, especially those who were co-dependent and/or who came from dysfunctional families. They seemed doomed to continue agonizing over making the changes to improve their life situation. Their apparent locking into their misery was astonishing. And yet, locking into misery is assured by the continual childhood experiences. Those negative experiences produced a series of attitudes and behaviors which prevent letting go of the misery, or developing defenses to help them make the changes. Instead, with the familiarity of dysfunction comes the locking into the misery. A main element of locking into misery is worry about making changes.

Misery Level

Determining your misery level is quite simple. If, for example, you dislike your boss but are being paid an excellent salary, you probably can withstand a fairly high level of misery, especially if you really don't think you can get the same pay elsewhere. Auto workers, for example, receive excellent pay and benefits, yet they complain a great deal about how miserable they feel. Unfortunately, as most are aware, they could not make as much money outside of the industry. As a result of this, very few leave.

Men and women in abusive relationships complain about how miserable they are. It never ceases to amaze me how much physical and emotional abuse someone will take. Certainly these people have a very high tolerance for misery.

To get more scientific about your actual misery level, try this exercise. List at least five things which, if you experienced them, would make you miserable. Rank them in order from the lowest to the highest misery level. Then write down what you feel is making you miserable now. Place it in the ranking. This will give you a relative value in comparison to the other items you have identified as miserable things. This level is important. You can begin to look at options for changing. When you do, your level of worry about the change becomes the dictating factor. This worry index will keep even the most miserable person hopelessly locked into the situation.

Worry Index

A simple device I invented to assess worry was the *Worry Index.* You can easily use it to see just how high your worry ranks and what effect it has in relation to your misery.

On a piece of paper, draw a horizontal line. Put numbers across it from 1 to 10, marking the area under the *1, low,* and under the *10, high.* See Figure 4.1.

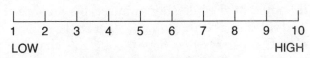

1	2	3	4	5	6	7	8	9	10
LOW									HIGH

Figure 4.1. Worry Index

Now assign a value to your present situation, that is, decide how worried you are about what is happening to you in the present. This will give you a focusing point for looking at other scenarios you might consider and their level of worry in relation to your present worry. We know most co-dependents are excellent worriers so this exercise should be easy to do, as well as essential. On the back of the paper, list as many alternative situations as you can. Regardless of their consequences, assign each of these new possibilities a value as to how much worry they would generate if you changed from your present situation to this new one. Mark its value on the Worry Index line as well. After you have done this for all your new possibilities, you will have a clear picture of your present worry index in relation to any other possible options.

After having hundreds of patients do this, I have found that any comparative situation which had a Worry Index spread of four points (present situation = 6; new situation = 10) rarely was considered as an alternative. A three point difference improved the likelihood of change about 30%. It wasn't until the change was seen as relatively the same as or less worrisome that a move was considered.

The impact of this information is important. You may have defined how miserable or unhappy you are in your present situation. You may even think that you can endure no more pain. But making the changes to feel better and stop the misery seems so frightening that you will remain locked into your present situation, continuing to be miserable.

Change Looks Good, But . . .

As we've seen, our misery is maintained much longer than it should be. People stay in miserable jobs, relationships and families as if they were galvanized to them. This is due to the worry they have about the changes that must take place before they can feel better. A change may look good on the surface but emotionally it's terrifying. Co-dependents, as a rule, have poor self-esteem, feel inadequate, have little experience caring about themselves and find it impossible to trust themselves or others.

Believing that they have the ability to make good decisions and survive, is even harder.

Although change may look good, co-dependents don't make those decisions. Co-dependents just don't feel they can risk. For them, change looks like a monster out there, just waiting to devour them. Most people avoid catastrophes if they can; co-dependents always avoid them. Catastrophic expectations will keep the co-dependent hopelessly addicted to misery.

Laboratory Experiments

1. Use the model in the *Misery Level* section. At the top of your paper, write what is making you the most miserable now in your life. Below that, identify and write five other things that, if you experienced them, would also make you miserable. Be sure to rank them. Decide where your present misery is in comparison to the five things you've listed.

2. Use the Worry Index model. Identify your present level of worry and alternatives. Plot these and get a better picture of what you're likely to risk and change. Now go back in time. Write down something that you were miserable about earlier in your life. Try to remember what things you worried about that kept you from changing. Plot these on another Worry Index. Then list the specific things you did that helped change your Worry Index and move on to the new situation.

3. Using your alternatives to make changes and reduce misery, think of ways to modify those options to lower worry and promote the likelihood of making the change.

FIVE

Expectations:
Catastrophic Versus Real

What Is Catastrophic, Anyway?

As far as I can determine, the word *catastrophe* has always meant something terrible. I learned the word as a child, watching a newscast of the *Andrea Doria* sinking. I recall hearing my father describe that event as "a terrible catastrophe which will cost the ship lines millions of dollars in lost business and lawsuits." My dad could always relate to things in economic terms. But my exposure to tragic events resulted in a clearer meaning of the term *catastrophic*. For the most part, I learned to avoid those situations where a catastrophe was imminent and I came to believe that most people did the same.

Those who are co-dependent and addicted to misery (ATM) have developed a very paradoxical relationship with catastrophe and catastrophic situations. Oftentimes, they are in what I define as catastrophic situations such as physically and/or emotionally abusive relationships. Yet at all costs they avoid changing or leaving those situations because of their perceived expectations that the change will produce a situation more catastrophic than their "real life." I've observed this many times in relationships which were emotionally dead. Neither partner was willing to make the first move and break it off. For them, it was the catastrophic expectation — "How am I going to make it outside of the relationship?" — that prevented them from leaving. Clearly it is important to understand where and how this process of developing catastrophic versus real expectations evolved.

Don't Blame Your Parents, Just Understand What Happened

The development of co-dependency explains why it is so resistant to treatment. Co-dependents learned early in life that there wasn't much of anything they could count on except that they couldn't count on much. Living with constant stress resulting from the dysfunction of an alcoholic, divorced, or emotionally repressive family, produced children who understood the need for using defenses to cope. The children in these families had to cope with rules that changed day to day, financial and emotional uncertainties and looking for ways to express emotions, only to be told, "You don't talk about feelings."

Rokelle Lerner, one of the founders of Children Are People, a program for prevention of chemical dependency in children, says that most of their perceptions are shattered. For them, the world is chaotic, out of control, not meaningful. This causes the development of a state of hypervigilance. Additionally, these children have grandiose expectations; but, more important, they develop co-dependent thinking and attitudes as a result of living with the catastrophic traumas produced by their families. Catastrophic trauma, unfortunately, is what the child comes to expect and before long, their level of comfort in making changes and adjustments in their lives becomes minimal, as their expectation of most changing situations is catastrophic. That sense of free-floating anxiety, which results from living in such unpredictable situations, makes taking chances and exploring other choices far too risky.

Understanding all this, as a child, is impossible. But recalling my own experiences and applying a little creative Hollywood drama, it began to make perfect sense. I related what was happening to old fears I had regarding my father's trips to Tokyo. His business made the visits to Japan mandatory and I recall that going there seemed very appealing. But I vowed never to make the trip.

Remembering Old Movies

I have grand memories of Saturday afternoon movie matinees when I was a boy. I recall sitting in the dimly lit theatre watching Godzilla, a 90 foot, fire-breathing dragon, come out of the earth after atomic bomb tests in the Arctic disrupted "nature's laws". In the movies, Godzilla always emerged from the volcano near Tokyo. I marveled that although the Army and the Air Force always tried to destroy Godzilla, he won every time. Each week he returned and smashed everything again. I swore back then never to live in or visit Tokyo. Let's face it, who wanted to go to a place where destruction and terror seemed certain? I saw those movies! Nothing stopped Godzilla until he had eaten his fill of people, smashed as many cars and buildings as he wanted, and did anything else he wished. All of these childhood fears existed in the face of what was a real conflict for me. As I indicated earlier, my father had been traveling to Japan for years, returning with wonderful gifts from Tokyo. He would tell stories that made life there sound terrific and he offered to take me along several times. It was only my Saturday matinee nightmares that kept me in this quandary. On the one hand, visiting Tokyo sounded like a kid's delight. Where else could one get so many small electronic things? On the other hand, what difference did it make if, while you were boarding the plane for home with all your wonderful trinkets, Godzilla arrived and began eating the plane and burning to a crisp all those who moved!

This Is Bad, But That's Worse

How does all this Godzilla business relate to co-dependency and addiction to misery? Simple. Co-dependents remain addicted to misery because of a basic learned fear, similar to mine of visiting Tokyo. Regardless of how desirable or attractive a new situation might be, when in the past most experiences involving change have produced painful or frightening results, the co-dependent's risking behavior will be minimal. Don't forget, I saw Godzilla eat everything. Unfortunately, those perceptions we experienced as children generally grow with us into adulthood and their permanence becomes difficult to dislodge.

Time and time again in therapy, I worked with co-dependent women who were in abusive relationships. The idea of leaving the relationship was catastrophic to them. A common response would be, "I know it's bad for the kids and me, but where would we go? How would we make it? I don't have a job that could support us. Besides, he only hits me when he's drunk." For her, staying in the relationship is bad, but leaving presents the worst-case scenario. It is this catastrophic expectation that she won't be able to make it, that galvanizes her to her present misery. If she leaves, Godzilla will certainly devour her and the children. What she has is bad, but changing or leaving certainly seems worse.

Co-dependents have an extreme lack of confidence in their ability to survive change. This will affect their recovery and keep them stuck and addicted to misery. There are two key elements which must be addressed if any improvement is to occur. The first is an intense fear of loss of control. Co-dependents grew up in environments where predictability and consistency didn't exist. This created a sense of free-floating anxiety such that the mere idea of change causes great discomfort, especially if it relates to basic human needs such as safety, food, clothing and shelter. Look at the anxiety dynamics of the co-dependent woman in the abusive relationship. Her basic needs were the very things threatened: shelter, survival, food.

The second element supporting both the co-dependency and addiction to misery is that staying miserable avoids catastrophic expectations. The co-dependent always expects the worst. "What I have may be miserable, but changing and risking is horrifying and not to be attempted."

How Big Is Godzilla?

These two notions work to keep the co-dependent addicted to misery. The therapeutic job is to convince the person that Godzilla is only 9 inches tall, not 90 feet and that although the changes to be made may at first look frightening and difficult, they can survive and move on with new choices and changes.

Lisa told a story of events which almost cost her life. She tried to avoid risking or making changes. Her co-dependent and ATM thinking was profound.

Lisa was a 26-year-old woman who had struggled for years with the problem of an extremely poor self-image. She came to therapy in a hyperanxious state. She had just finalized her second divorce and told me she had barely escaped with her life. The story was almost unbelievable. After months of physical abuse, one night while she slept, her husband poured gasoline on her. Her brother was staying with the couple at the time and successfully overpowered the husband just as he was about to ignite her. This marriage occurred only three months after her first ended and that one also included physical and verbal abuse for nearly five years. Lisa was not the type of person I would have expected to endure this lifestyle. She was not uneducated, social deprived, chemically depen-dent or financially destitute. In fact, she held an impressive position with a major corporation, made excellent money, and looked like a model on the cover of a fashion magazine. She held an MBA in Business Administration and was articulate and intelligent. Her present distress, which was also causing many physical symptoms, focused around the fear that her present boyfriend had all the characteristics of her past two husbands. In our early sessions, I asked if she had ever dated men who were less physical or who treated her with kindness and sensitivity. She replied, "Men like that turn me off, especially the nice ones. I've tried them and been bored. I seem to have an energy level that never goes away and needs 'crazy'. I guess I'm just attracted to the misery." The concept of attraction just didn't fit. All the elements of addiction were present. In this case, it seemed that addiction to misery was a more appropriate explanation.

In treating Lisa, the primary objective with regard to her revelation that she was addicted to having the same miserable relationships over and over, was to convince her that letting go of a relationship once it proved unsatisfying, and especially if it was punitive, would not force her into a state of celibacy and chronic loneliness; and that she had good potential for sensitive and caring relationships without all the soap opera dramatics of her previous ones. This was the main focus of her therapy.

Feeling Good, Having Success
And Winning — Not For Me

Misery addicts have very little experience with feeling good. This does not refer to feeling good physically, but emotionally. Early childhood traumas and situations prepared us to expect a lot of disappointments and sadness, such that when a success or good feeling comes along, we seem almost to wish it away. Sometimes it appears that we purposely sabotage the success or good feeling because we are so unfamiliar with it.

One of my best "Feeling good, having success, and winning . . . that's not for me" clients was Bill.

At 35, Bill had been hospitalized a second time for alcoholism. He had problems with alcohol for nearly 20 years — legal, financial, job, family and health problems. Unmanageability and powerlessness were both features of his addiction. Shortly after his first discharge from treatment, he was preparing to remarry. Upon returning to work, he received a promotion. His health improved greatly and, overall, his life was better than it had ever been. Best of all, he had stopped drinking, a feat previously unattainable. Three months after his discharge, with the new marriage, improved health and job situation, Bill returned to drinking. The simple conclusion to be drawn was that he was still in denial of his alcoholism. However, after assessing and evaluating him during his second admission, something in addition was present beyond mere denial, delusion or ignorance of his illness. In the interview, when I asked him why he returned to drinking, he replied, "Doc, things were just going too damn good." It was clear that what he meant was that familiarity with good feelings and success didn't exist. His experience with being miserable was undoubtedly more familiar and, as crazy as it seemed, more comfortable for him. He appeared driven to sabotage his successes, just as he had done throughout his life. Addiction to misery was his orientation and the notion of leaving this state was intolerable.

For this man, the state of winning, being successful or feeling good just didn't exist. He was addicted to misery and all of those positive elements just didn't fit, for him.

Laboratory Experiments

1. The rules of dysfunctional families usually include: *don't talk; don't trust;* and, *don't feel.* Try to recall if and how these messages were given to you and by whom. Write out the specific rules in your home and their effects on you as a child. See if you can make the connection of their effect in your adult life. An example might be: As a child, you did not learn to trust grown-ups; as an adult, you find it very difficult to trust anyone.

2. Describe your present (or most recent) miserable situation. Then explain, as clearly as possible, why you remain(ed) in that situation. Be sure to identify the "It's bad" part; then the "But that's worse" part that keeps you from changing.

3. Look at the experiences in your life which could be classified as feeling good, having success, being a winner. Ask yourself if those experiences lasted, and if they didn't, why not? Did you play a part in their ending? If so, how?

SIX

Self-Victimization

Most modern child psychologists and experts in early child development would agree that the experiences of our early years make lasting impressions on the way we behave, think and feel as adults and how we perceive the world around us. Children of dysfunctional families, abusive, alcoholic or divorced, have learned many unfortunate things about themselves and their environment. In Chapter 3, we discussed the familiar versus unfamiliar experiences of a child in a dysfunctional family. Paramount among the results of these experiences, is that the child comes to feel victimized by his parents. When things go wrong in the outside world (school, friends, etc.), he sees this victimization as generic, that is, applying to everywhere. "People don't like me." It doesn't take long, then, to think, "I'm not very good," or "I might as well not try, it's going to go wrong anyway."

This self-defeating attitude goes on to affect the way we see ourselves, enter into relationships and live out the role of victim. Even young children who feel victimized look for people to rescue or help. These are attempts to redeem themselves from their poor self-image. Trying to please an alcoholic parent becomes an obsessive need in order to receive any acknowledgment or acceptance. Rokelle Lerner talks about the "getting days." Kids from these families know they must not ask for much when their parent is drinking or drugging and they carefully plan the times they know they can ask. The "getting days" are the ones when they can get some acceptance and caring, little as it may be. This complicated and unpredictable system creates children who grow up feeling victimized and tremendously insecure. A victimized child, living in an adult body, is a sitting duck to enter one sick relationship after another. We become expertly prepared to play two psychosocial roles: the *rescuer*, and the *victim*.

Drama Triangle

Stephen Karpman devised what he called the Karpman Drama Triangle to explain the roles we take on in relationships and the kind of people we look for to be involved with. In the triangle (see Figure 6.1), rescuers engage themselves with victims. Strange as it may seem, this odd-couple really fit each other quite well. Rescuers need people to save or rescue and victims look for people to save them. But therein lies a problem. Victims look for people to feel sorry for them and give them sympathy and rarely want someone telling them what to do. The role of victim requires one to remain a victim, so anything that would threaten that would be strongly opposed. On the other hand, rescuers never feel satisfied or fulfilled unless they are able to rid the victim of his problems. For most rescuers, this is the primary way to derive self-worth and when the rescuer is denied his rescuing because victims never really want to be fixed, the rescuer feels defeated, inadequate and generally worse than before the helping attempts.

When the rescuer stops trying to fix or rescue the victim, this apparent rule change angers and scares the victim, for without the rescuer, who will listen or give sympathy? What is more important, who will the victim have to control and manipulate, if the rescuer leaves that role? In an attempt to pull the rescuer back into place on the triangle, the victim shifts to the role of persecutor. Using threats and overt gestures, oftentimes the victim is able to manipulate the rescuer back onto the triangle, so as to assume his own role of victim once again.

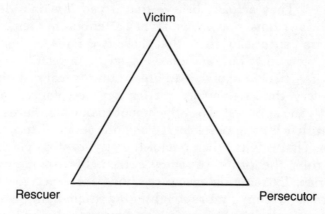

Figure 6.1. Drama Triangle

It would be insulting to assert that men and women who marry one alcoholic after another are doing so because they want to. Yet it is uncanny how many people do this. The two conditions and characteristics described in the Drama Triangle seem to lend a reasonable explanation for this repetitious choosing of one bad relationship after another. Rescuers are people with a mission. They seek out people they can feel sorry for and think, "They need my help." The key element is that they have attached their self-worth to the success of others. I've always joked with my rescuing clients that they are like Boy Scouts looking for little old ladies to walk across the street. No merit badges (recognition) unless they do. But, I point out, there are not enough little old ladies in all the world for the badge they are trying to earn, that of unconditional acceptance and approval. Therefore, they will always fail.

Victims, too, have a mission. They go through life looking eternally for recognition of their tragic plight. Everybody and everything has gone wrong for them and they keep trying to find people who will hear their cry and lend sympathy. When they meet someone who suggests changes to end their misery, they quickly discount them and look elsewhere. Their self-worth is poor, but improving it removes their ability to gain any acceptance as victims. They actually believe that if people didn't view them as victims, nobody would pay attention to them.

It isn't surprising then, that these two types of people seek each other out, and once engaged in a relationship, find it virtually impossible to break out, for fear of losing the very things they need: attention, acceptance, self-worth and approval. The attachment to one another is so great that leaving poses incredible interpersonal security risks. That is why when one of the players stops playing his role, the other becomes extremely anxious and worried. Extreme defensive reactions are expected and there is nothing more frightening than living with someone who has stopped playing by the rules or being predictable. When a partner in the relationship steps off the Drama Triangle, emotional recovery begins. However, without support and help, people used to living on the triangle either return to it or go out and look for other partners to play with them. This perpetuates the unhappiness, which feeds the addiction to misery.

<u>Laboratory Experiments</u>

1. Look at the Drama Triangle. Identify the role you have played and with whom. Determine if you play one role more often than others. Describe if and how you have or might stop and get off the triangle.

SEVEN

Disavowing Painful Reality: Denial

Regardless of where I go or whom I see, it seems all of us, when faced with something we don't choose to experience, will disavow painful reality, that is, we deny. Denying a reality when it is painful is normal; in fact, it works as a defense mechanism to assist us in actually learning to deal with painful reality.

Elisabeth Kübler-Ross, in her book, *On Death and Dying,* spoke of the emotional process she observed in people dealing with grief. She identified five stages we go through in the grieving process: denial; anger; bargaining; depression; and acceptance. The person suffering from grief can only move on or feel better after he passes through the first four stages and progresses to acceptance — acceptance, not only of the situation, but of his own feelings about it.

Kübler-Ross saw the grieving process extended by two things: being stuck in the cycle and not crossing over to acceptance; and trying to deny the basic feelings about the death. In many cases, misery addicts and co-dependents struggle similarly. Their grieving comes from all the losses they experienced in their dysfunctional childhoods, like loss of safety, loss of rituals, loss of spirituality, loss of boundaries, loss of friendships, and the most important loss of all, the loss of memories. Dealing in adult situations without those experiences makes us feel that much more lost. ATMs and co-dependents have storehouses of hurt and pain that need processing, not to open up old wounds but to let out what has never been dealt with.

A young woman I worked with had kept inside herself for many years the pain and hurt of her father's sexual abuse. To deal with that tragedy, she turned to drugs and alcohol. She also put herself in one abusive relationship after another. She had made several attempts at sobriety, returning to chemicals after each treatment. When I met her, she was in her fourth treatment. Once she was past the detoxification period, we began looking carefully at her relapse patterns. Each time, there were clear associations with the men she had had relationships with. As noted, each one involved abuse. This seemed so similar to her tragic childhood that she looked for any way to escape the pain. She had disavowed the painful reality of her past long enough and had to begin to address those haunting emotional issues.

Defended by nothing, angry at everything, this woman was not only chemically dependent but severely addicted to misery. After some trusting began to bond in treatment, she told us of how diligently she worked as a little girl to protect her father from her mother's accusations. Finally, when her father walked out, her mother just quit mothering and she became the primary caretaker of her three younger brothers. For her, the role of rescuer fit perfectly. She sought out men who cried the blues and played the victims. The perfect match! Recovery from drugs and alcohol was easy; follow the 12-Step program and attend AA and NA meetings. But recovery from her addiction to misery and co-dependent thinking was clearly more difficult. First, she would have to understand why she hurt and make peace with the reality that it wasn't her fault, a burden she had carried for a long time. This treatment was different for her. Besides developing standard treatment plans for drugs and alcohol, several were created to address her specific ATM and co-dependent ways.

Specific assignments addressing repression of feelings and denial were given. The concept of attachment was explained to her and she wrote an essay describing the way she would attach herself to people, especially men, and how she only let go after taking significant abuse. We began to teach her ways to care for herself and pointed out how to begin detaching. We used a symbolic exercise to rid her of the terrible guilt and anger she had felt since childhood about her sexual abuse. She was instructed to write her father a letter describing all her feelings, both then and through the years. Then she was told to burn it and let it go. The process of disavowing painful reality had ended. Today, after two years, she remains sober, continues to work her recovery program and is no longer co-dependent or addicted to misery.

Wanting To Get Better

ATMs want to get better. Often, it is easy to see what is causing their misery, yet relieving the misery is not easy. ATMs have pre-existing developmental impairments such as repression of feelings, obsessive-compulsive thoughts and behaviors, catastrophic expectations of change and familiarity with unhappiness. These things act in ways to block and prevent change. Wanting to get better isn't enough. And, even when life gets better, our experience with the "better" is so unfamiliar that we find "better" uncomfortable and even miserable. The basic system which supports the addiction needs to be identified, understood, accepted and, finally, changed before the pain can stop.

Like all addicts, ATMs look for ways to medicate their distress. They continue to disavow painful reality and avoid change.

Medicators: Do They Really Help?

Misery addicts look for ways to keep from feeling lonely, inadequate, shy, scared, guilty, in any way uncomfortable. They want to put those feelings to sleep or to numb them. This is usually much easier than dealing with them and making the changes to stop the pain. Numbing feelings and stopping the pain is done by medicating, in the same way the dentist numbs or medicates your gums before he drills your tooth. This is a temporary halt; as we know, when the medicator wears off, your mouth still hurts. For our purposes, medicators include alcohol, drugs, food, sex, cigarettes, work, money or anything that is used as a way of coping until one is ready to risk and make changes to stop the pain.

Ridding oneself of the medicators lets the feelings come out. Their ability to survive the processing of feelings is probably the single most important revelation for ATMs. That emotional expectation system that says, "You won't survive," must be challenged and denied. Living with feelings is necessary to recover from addiction to misery, even though our past dictates so much of what we think and how we act. Major obstacles must be confronted to stop the pain, accept the reality and move on from the misery.

The reminder that misery's absence is going to feel unfamiliar, uncomfortable and at times miserable, needs to be a constant part of our recovery. Misery and our familiarity with it evolved over a long period of time. The journey of becoming familiar with its absence will also be long.

Laboratory Experiments

1. Identify the losses you had as a child, e.g., loss of safety, boundaries, ritual, spirituality, friendships, memories, etc. Try to connect each of these losses to yourself as an adult and see how you carried each one over. As an example, if you felt, as a child, that you never really had boundaries, describe how you may still have a problem following directions.
2. Describe clearly and in as much detail as you can, the specific events and memories you have tried to forget. Remember, writing or talking about something can never be as painful as actually living through the experience. Then see how you have let those experiences affect your relationships with others, your attitudes and beliefs.
3. List the medicators you have used and continue to use to deal with pain.
4. If there remains a tragic pain in your memory, write a letter to the person who hurt you. Be sure to describe how you felt, but don't make this a hate letter. Then burn it, letting go of the pain with the ashes.

EIGHT

Feeling Good, But It Won't Last

Over and over again I've heard misery addicts say, "When things are going well, I don't expect it to last," or "When things are going badly, I expected it." These two notions feed the ATMs' expectation system and lock out emotional optimism.

This becomes the real focus of the misery addict's recovery. We can be taught to stop the co-dependent thinking and behaviors. Our co-dependency ends when we stop trying to control others, repress our feelings, worry about everybody and everything, and start caring about ourselves. This will take time but IT CAN BE ACCOMPLISHED. Unfortunately, our co-dependent thinking and behaving didn't evolve in a few weeks, months, or even years of crazy experiences. Instead, it evolved over a long period of time. In some cases, it existed during our entire childhood and adolescence, and with the co-dependence came a feeling of long-standing misery. Now imagine that the co-dependency stops, self-caring begins and life feels great. What experience base do we have to deal with this? Our waiting-for-the-ax-to-fall philosophy is as much a part of us as our skin. Thoughts like, "It feels so great to be away from the insanity, but I'm so afraid it won't last," are normal for misery addicts.

Our familiarity with feeling good and having things go right is generally so limited, that we tend to experience a feeling of discomfort which soon is just as bad as the feelings of misery and co-dependency were. Sounds crazy! It happens all the time. Recovery from co-dependency occurs but the unfamiliarity of feeling good is so powerful that we end up worrying about its lasting, or looking for ways to leave it and return to the misery.

Carly Simon, in her hit song, *I Haven't Got Time For The Pain*, speaks so clearly to what ATMs and co-dependents believe, that suffering is the price of survival. The words say that we came to expect bad things and we have to suffer just to survive. Addicts of misery expect it and actually nurture it. When it's absent, things feel unfamiliar, or worse, "wrong." But our misery only stops when we take the responsibility to stop our pain and start recovering.

ATM Philosophy

ATMs and co-dependents share similar philosophies. Both are *other*-oriented, meaning that they believe responsibility for what happens to them is based on what others do. They share a pessimistic approach to life.

"'When others change, things will get better." This other-than-myself thinking is at the heart of the ATM's belief system. By passing the responsibility to others to maintain or make changes which will affect us, we keep ourselves in their control: *If he would only tell me I am wonderful. If I didn't always have to please her. Why can't they ever be happy with me? They never like what I do.*

These power/controlling words take away our own control over the feelings we have about ourselves. Every time I give someone else the power to approve, recognize, validate or judge me, I lose power over the way I think about myself. We all look for these things from people but I am specifically addressing the way ATMs and co-dependents habitually look to others for self-validation. When we talked about the Karpman Drama Triangle, we saw that our poor skills in choosing relationships makes the potential mentors we select to learn and receive acknowledgment from, are the least likely to support us. Instead, we get ridicule, put-downs, blame, rejection, victimization and a sense of never being good enough.

The belief that when others change, things will get better must be denied. Instead, our belief must become "When we change, things will get better." Our responsibility for our behaviors and happiness must be defined clearly. Ridding ourselves of the emotional-philosophical dependency is difficult but essential if our misery addiction is to end.

Self-Talk And Lifestyles

I worked with a man who told me his philosophy: "You can't trust anybody! Anyone who gives me something must want something. Don't tell anyone your business — it's none of theirs. I've been this way all my life and I don't want to change."

These reclusive, repressive, almost paranoid attitudes are typical of ATMs and many co-dependents. This man's approach to life is basic to breeding chronic unhappiness, distrust and misery, as though he were living in the classic W.C. Fields movie, *Never Give A Sucker An Even Break*. If you give in, someone will certainly be waiting to take advantage of you. I have worked with hundreds of people of all ages who have these views. They all share one common denominator: They all come from dysfunctional families.

You can see how these feelings and attitudes about life will affect your day-to-day life. You become very limited in what you do. Venturing out or taking risks of any kind is rare. Dealing with emotions and feelings occurs only internally, making you subject to explosiveness. Irrational behavior is the way you defend yourself against confrontational situations. In general, it is a lifestyle of disassociation, repression, loneliness and misery.

Laboratory Experiments

1. Make a list of the good experiences or feelings you have had in the past year or so. Indicate if you felt they would last, and if not, why.
2. Look at the section, *ATM Philosophy*. List the power/control words you use to make you dependent on others for feeling good. Describe what must happen to stop feeling bad and what your responsibility is.
3. Write out your daily self-talk. Explain how it keeps you addicted to misery.

NINE

Breaking The Addiction

Recovery from any addiction requires abstinence from the thing we are addicted to. Alcoholics and drug addicts must abstain from all mood-altering chemicals. Eating-disordered people must stop their addictive eating behaviors. Gamblers must stop gambling and co-dependents must abstain from trying to control others.

The key to all recovery is caring about yourself. Beyond *taking care of* yourself, you must begin to *care for* yourself. I heard Robert Ackerman, author of *Let Go and Grow*, say one time, "Stop doing what you don't do." Before recovery, addicts don't ask for help. Stop doing that! They don't go to self-help groups or get sponsors. Stop doing that! They don't say what they mean or mean what they say. Stop doing that! Mainly, they don't care about themselves. Stop doing that!

Misery addicts have to abstain from those situations which support the misery. Worry is to the misery addict what alcohol is to the alcoholic. The more worry, the worse the misery. As I have said over and over, the basis for recovery is admitting the problem and then understanding the causal connection between the pain of the addiction and the obstacles preventing recovery.

You can't begin to dismantle misery thinking until you can clearly identify the pain it is causing. Earnie Larson, author of many books on recovery and co-dependency, talks in his book, *Stage II Recovery*, about how we never move on from our pain until we're ready to make peace with reality, make peace with ourselves and let go. I see this with misery addicts all the time. Elements of addiction such as denial and repression of feelings keep the addict from ever looking at the reality he must face. When he is ready to look at and accept reality, the pain stops and the misery ends.

Steps To Dismantle Miserable Thinking

The first step in dismantling the kind of thinking that reinforces misery addiction is to identify what I call *miserable thoughts*. These are ideas which make us unhappy, sad, depressed, worried, scared, or to have other negative feelings.

The second step is understanding. Trying to dismantle miserable thoughts without understanding how they were conceived is just plain frustrating. Chapter 3 identified the ways in which miserable thinking is developed. You may want to go back and re-read the chapter to help you understand the origins of this thinking.

The next step is to redefine our reality. For so long, we have looked at our misery as something to be expected. We came to expect things to be the way they were because of our past experiences. A child from a dysfunctional home doesn't grow up expecting life to be smooth and wonderful. Quite the contrary. Those chaotic childhood experiences made us expect that when things are going well, it won't last, and when things are going badly, it's just normal.

We need to see reality as "Things can go right and when things don't, it won't last." We must look for more positive ways to see things and finally, we must find and work at ways to leave the pain.

The process of beginning to care about ourselves is the next step. After we have redefined reality, we must look for ways to forgive ourselves. How often have we blamed ourselves for misery when in actuality, we didn't cause it. This final step affords us an opportunity to make peace with ourselves. It is a way to let go of our miserable thinking once and for all and to stop blaming ourselves.

Identify And Remove The Medicators

In the process of dismantling the thinking which supports our addiction to misery we must look for the ways in which we cope with our distress. We have to know those things we use to stop the misery. Recovery can't start until the medicators are gone. If we continue to drink, drug, eat, not eat, smoke, etc., as a way to disavow painful reality, we only perpetuate the misery. Our medicating must stop and we need healthy emotional ways out of the misery.

Begin Risk-Taking

Probably the single most powerful change we must make is to begin risk-taking. Looking at ways to change our misery generally requires us to risk, and as you know, if we expect Godzilla to eat us up, we will never make it out the door. After our miserable thinking is dismantled, our realities changed, our medicators removed, risk-taking is easier.

We are reminded too well of the times we tried to make changes by risking new behaviors, only to have them end in tragedy. These experiences are the most important ones which shape our present responses. Again, we must understand our past to explain and begin to change our present.

We must look at the things which we see as changes needed to move away from misery and then clearly define the risks. Write them out. Talk with friends or people who can support you to see if they view your risks as you do. Often, our catastrophic expectations are so unrealistic and unreasonable that we need others to help us see that. We can calibrate our risk-taking and scale it up or down by doing more, or less, to change our misery. First of all, we must reduce our catastrophic thinking so as to free ourselves to take the risks and make the changes.

A.W.A.R.E. — *Able, Willing And Ready To Exchange*

Misery addiction is not much different than any other addiction when it comes to recovery. The basic steps on the road to recovery are the same.

I developed an acronym which I gave to clients on a card as a constant reminder of what they needed to do to recover: A.W.A.R.E.

A. *Able:* We must be able to look our problem in the face and see that we can make the necessary changes to recover.

W. *Willing:* We must be willing to make whatever changes are needed for our recovery.

A.R. *And Ready:* We must be ready to live with temporary discomfort in order to recover.

E. *Exchange:* We must exchange our old thinking, attitudes and behaviors for the new ones of recovery.

Our awareness of our ability to survive, of what we're willing to do, and our readiness to change, put us on the firmest ground to begin recovery from addiction to misery.

Laboratory Experiments

1. To help dismantle miserable thinking, list as many miserable thoughts as you can. After each, write out what you understand about its origins. Where did this thinking come from? You may have to go back to your experiences as a young child. Describe the realities that might replace your miserable thoughts. Finally, list ways in which you might forgive yourself if you selfishly made changes that others might not like.

2. List the medicators you use to deal with feelings. Begin with what you use to deal with anger, sadness, fear, boredom and loneliness. Now add any other feelings and medicators.

3. Write out the specific risks involved with changes to leave misery. Ask others to tell you ways to reduce the risks and help lower your anxiety about making the changes.

4. Make your own **A.W.A.R.E.** card. Carry it with you for one week. As you experience situations which make you miserable, use your **A.W.A.R.E.** card to remind you of your ability to make changes and stop the misery.

TEN

Recovery — A Here And Now Process

I sat listening to a client, one morning, tell me the many reasons why she was miserable. She had been living with an alcoholic husband for many, many years and recently quit work for health reasons. She wanted to feel better but was unwilling to change. For her, every option for change had a *what if* attached to it. For example: *What if* I left my husband, and my family was upset? *What if* my children don't want me to leave? *What if* I can't change to make them happy? *What if* I get a job I don't like? *What if* I have to move from my house? *What if? What if? What if?*

Finally, I said to her, "So what!" Nothing she was saying to me had the potential to cause more misery than she was already in. In fact, I was certain most of the changes she needed would result in less misery. I had to convince her of that. Living with *what ifs* cripples our chances of leaving our misery addiction. For meaningful recovery, we must step into the here and now. The process of leaving our painful past prepares us for the experiences we must cope with in the present. This here and now process is the main element in our recovery. If we continue to use the past to predict the outcomes of our present and future, we might just as well remain there in the misery. At the very least, we need to declare an emotional neutrality which says: "I'm not going to use the experiences of my past to predict how successful I will be in my changes." This neutrality is so important that without it, we will fail to find any relief. It will prevent us from reaching the here and now stage to address the issues of recovery.

Basics Of Recovery

People who are co-dependent and addicted to misery believe their plight will improve only when others change. This belief system, that of being convinced that "I can't feel better" or, "Things won't change for me until others change" must be removed. The premise that others are responsible for our happiness and are the only possibility for things to improve, is what treatment must address. Melody Beattie, in *Co-Dependent No More*, talks about taking our hands out of other people's emotional pockets and putting them back into our own. Recovery doesn't begin until this process starts.

As we saw earlier, we must start challenging our denial system. This means giving up the medicators that prevent change. Once this is in process, the emotional system begins to recover and wake up. Surrendering to powerlessness is probably the most difficult stage of recovery for co-dependents and persons addicted to misery. Feelings are finally beginning to emerge, and there is a re-identification of ourselves as the ones in power over what we do. With this realization comes the pain and frustration that "I really don't know how to take care of myself. I feel sad, hurt and angry and I don't know what to do." We come face to face with our recognition that although others may cause the pain, hurt, fear, disrespect, etc., it is our own power and control that keeps us in those situations. I am amazed at how little we credit our own survivability, which has allowed us to make it for so long. My client had taken care of her husband, raised her children and worked most of her life. Yet she was questioning her ability to take care of herself. Her *what ifs* of the future and, as she put it, "failures of the past to fix things" had kept her addicted to misery. She had never been able to get into the present, the here and now.

Here And Now

Why is recovery a here and now process? Let's look at some reasons. At the heart of AA's recovery program is the admonition to take things "one day at a time." Over and over, patients ask, "Why do this?" Of greater concern is, "How can I do this?"

The why of living life one day at a time is fairly simple. If I stay in the present (here and now), I greatly reduce the number of situations which can cause imbalance, that is, there are fewer distractions. It is easier to maintain emotional balance in the course of a day, rather than a week, a month or a year. Also, I stop worrying about the outcome of future unknowns. Predicting the future is not particularly satisfying and certainly becomes stressful, and it sets us up for disappointments.

Living one day at a time (here and now) is not easy, but the most important thing you can do is to stop predicting. Make plans, explore opportunities, set goals. But, don't attempt to predict the outcomes. Repeat!! Don't predict the outcomes. Deal with what you know, not what you think. By doing this, you greatly reduce worry, frustration, anxiety and fear of what you can't control. Getting into the here and now gives you back your power and control over what you can change today. This is so important to recovery.

Past-ing And Futuring

These are two terms I invented to describe what ATMs and co-dependents do. Simple to understand, yet hard to change.

Past-ing is a process of using the past as a way to affect everything today. Here's how it works. Take something that goes wrong or shows our limitations, something like losing a job, or breaking up a relationship. Truly, these are significant events in and of themselves. Yet, we would expect to recover and move on. ATMs and co-dependents come to the table of life with many feelings of inadequacy; they feel incompetent and worthless. As we said, this comes from the earliest experiences in our families-of-origin. We would expect to take these situations very personally. When things go wrong, ATMs and co-dependents magnify the wrong by attaching it mentally to all those other experiences in their past. This magnifies the effect tenfold. This is what I call past-ing, an emotionally crippling device which holds back our thinking and ability to move on.

Futuring is a process whereby we become so worried about what's going to happen that it disables us from making changes to end our misery. ATMs and co-dependents do this all the time. It fits the *what-if* syndrome and stops change. When we become paralyzed in the present (here and now) due to futuring, we can't move on; we remain stuck.

These two notions act like terrorists on a plane, holding you captive and not allowing you to proceed. We either have the memories of the past to increase our present pain, or worry so about what the future might be with change, that misery remains. This cycle must be broken. Identifying, understanding, removing medicators and beginning to take risks are necessary steps to end addiction to misery. Becoming **A.W.A.R.E.** and using the technique to exchange old thinking, behaving and attitudes, starts the recovery, removes the pain, creates new hope and ends the misery.

I Can Make It

This book was written to help us look more openly and honestly at ourselves than we've previously been willing to do, to give ourselves the maps and tools we need to leave the misery we've had for so long. I wanted to stop the feelings of inadequacy, worry, loneliness, guilt and shame for a long time. My best friends were therapists, psychologists, psychiatrists and social workers. Advice from them was easily given yet rarely followed. It wasn't until I understood how I got the thoughts and feelings about myself that I could even begin to see why the misery lasted so long. My family were good people who cared in the best way they could, but they only knew what they learned. My needs for acceptance and approval seemed insatiable and I could never figure out why. No one ever made me feel or think the way I did but I developed my own coping process. To avoid disappointment, I would do anything. In that process, I remained locked into one miserable life situation after another. A therapist finally said to me one day, "Congratulations, Rob. You've finally hung up your suit of armor. No more dragon-slaying or rescuing damsels in distress." I knew what she meant because for the first time in my life, I began to care for myself, care for others and stop trying to take care of others. The changes happened because I came to believe I'm important, I'm competent and I can make it.

God bless you, and you can too!

APPENDIX A

Where To Look For Help

Seeking out the support of others who have had experiences similar to our own makes sense. People who have lived with, or are now in, dysfunctional situations can share your fears, frustrations, co-dependencies and, most assuredly, your misery. As pointed out here, those addicted to misery (ATMs) can be found in alcoholic, drug-dependent, divorced, physically and mentally abusive, eating-disordered or any emotionally repressive family or relationship. There are specific self-help groups to assist people living — or surviving — in one of these situations. Contact a group office in your area (see the white pages of your local phone book) to get their meeting schedule. If you do not find a listing in your local phone book, consult the resource list in Appendix B for the headquarters address and inquire there for a group near you.

Other self-help groups have flourished in the past few years, run by professional therapists. Often these groups are low in cost and generally less expensive than individual therapy.

One of the most important things that belonging to a support group does is to remove your sense of isolation. Knowing you're not the only one who has a given problem can greatly reduce the fear that things can't or won't ever change. ATMs struggle with this problem the most. Support groups de-fuse the idea that change is worse than remaining in a painful situation. The catastrophic scenario is often diminished merely by seeing other individuals who have made the changes and have survived, moving on in life and away from misery.

Many companies today offer employees and their family members counseling services and referrals through their Employee Assistance Programs (EAPs). EAP counselors have specific training to deal with dependencies of all types and they usually have referral resources to help with specific problems.

APPENDIX B

Resources

Addiction Research Foundation
33 Russell Street
Toronto, Ontario
Canada M55 2S1

Adult Children of Alcoholics
6381 Hollywood Blvd., Suite 685
Hollywood, CA 90028

Al-Anon/Alateen Family Group Headquarters, Inc.
P.O. Box 862, Midtown Station
New York, NY 10018-0862
(212) 302-7240

Alcoholics Anonymous (AA)
P.O. Box 459, Grand Central Station
New York, NY 10163-1100

American Anorexia/Bulimia Association, Inc.
133 Cedar Lane
Teaneck, NJ 07666
(201) 836-1800

American Humane Association
Children's Division
P.O. Box 1266
Denver, CO 80201
(303) 695-0811

Batterers Anonymous
Box 29
Redlands, CA 92373

Catholic Family and Children's Services
(See the white pages of your local phone book.)

Center for Women Policy Studies
2000 P Street N.W. — Suite 508
Washington, DC 20036
(202) 872-1770
(Information about services and programs for battered children,
battered women and men who batter is available through this
center.)

Child Care Information Center
532 Settlers Landing Road
P.O. Box 548
Hampton, VA 23669
(804) 722-4495

Child Welfare League of America, Inc.
67 Irving Place
New York, NY 10003
(212) 254-7410

Childhelp USA's National Child Abuse Hotline
(800) 4-A-CHILD

Children Are People, Inc.
493 Selby Avenue
St. Paul, MN 55102
(612) 227-4031

Children of Alcoholics Foundation, Inc.
200 Park Avenue, 31st floor
New York, NY 10166
(212) 949-1404

Children of Alcoholics: The New Jersey Task Force
P.O. Box 190
Rutherford, NJ 07070
(201) 460-7912

Co-dependents Anonymous
Central Office: P.O. Box 5508
Glendale, AZ 85312-5508
(602) 944-0141 (1:00 to 5:00 p.m.)

Community Interventions, Inc.
220 South Tenth Street
Minneapolis, MN 55403
(612) 332-6537

Debtors Anonymous
Box 20322
New York, NY 10025-9992

Divorce Anonymous
Box 5313
Chicago, IL 60680

Emotions Anonymous
Box 4245
St. Paul, MN 55104

Families Anonymous
Box 344
Torrance, CA 90501

Families in Action
Suite 300
3845 North Druid Hills Road
Decatur, GA 30033

Family Service Agency, Inc.
(See the white pages of your local phone book.)

Gamanon
Box 967, Radio City Station
New York, NY 10019

Gamblers Anonymous
Box 17173
Los Angeles, CA 90017

Incest Survivors Anonymous
Box 5613
Long Beach, CA 90805

Jewish Family and Children's Services
(See the white pages of your local phone book.)

Lutheran Family and Children's Services
(See the white pages of your local phone book.)

Nar-Anon Family Groups
350 5th Street, Suite 207
San Pedro, CA 90731

Narcotics Anonymous
Box 9999
Van Nuys, CA 91409

National Association for Adult Children of Alcoholics
31582 Coast Highway, Suite B
Laguna Beach, CA 92677

National Association of Anorexia Nervosa and
  Associated Disorders
P.O. Box 7
Highland Park, IL 60035
(312) 831-3438

National Association for Children of Alcoholics
13706 Coast Highway, Suite 201
South Laguna, CA 92677

National Clearinghouse for Alcohol Information
P.O. Box 2345
Rockville, MD 20850
(301) 468-2600

National Clearinghouse on Marital Rape
Women's History Research Center
2325 Oak Street
Berkeley, CA 94708

National Coalition against Domestic Violence
1500 Massachusetts Avenue N.W., Suite 35
Washington, DC 20036
(Information about programs for men who batter is available
through this organization. Most states have statewide coalitions
working against domestic violence which can be contacted in
state capitals.)

National Council on Alcoholism
12 West 21st Street, 7th floor
New York, NY 10010

National Exchange Club Foundation for the
  Prevention of Child Abuse
(419) 535-3232

National Institute on Alcohol Abuse and Alcoholism
5600 Fishers Lane
Rockville, MD 20857
(301) 443-2403

National Single Parent Coalition
10 West 23rd Street
New York, NY 10010

Other Victims of Alcoholism, Inc.
P.O. Box 921, Radio City Station
New York, NY 10019
(212) 247-8087

Overeaters Anonymous
P.O. Box 92870
Los Angeles, CA 90009
(213) 542-8363

Overeaters Anonymous
4025 Spenser Street, Suite 203
Torrance, CA 90503

Parental Stress Service, Inc.
154 Santa Clara Avenue
Oakland, CA 95610
(415) 841-1750

Parents Anonymous — National Office
22330 Hawthorne
Torrance, CA 90505

Parents Without Partners
7910 Woodmont Avenue
Washington, DC 20014

Pill-Anon Family Programs
Box 120, Gracie Station
New York, NY 10028

Pills Anonymous
Box 473, Ansonia Station
New York, NY 10023

Prison Families Anonymous
134 Jackson Street
Hempstead, NY 11550

Rutgers Center of Alcohol Studies
P.O. Box 969
Piscataway, NJ 08854
(201) 932-2190

Shelter Aid
(800)-333-SAFE

Single Dad's Hotline
Box 4842
Scottsdale, AZ 85258

Survivors Network
18653 Ventura Boulevard #143
Tarzana, CA 91356

United Way Crisis Line/Information and Referral
(See the white pages of your local phone book.)

APPENDIX C

Recommended Reading

Ackerman, R. J., **Children of Alcoholics: A Guidebook for Educators, Therapists, and Parents,** (2nd Ed.). Holmes Beach, Florida: Learning Publications, 1983.

Ackerman, R. J., (edited by), **Growing in the Shadow: Children of Alcoholics,** Pompano Beach, Florida: Health Communications, 1986.

Ackerman, R. J., **Let Go and Grow,** Pompano Beach, Florida: Health Communications, 1987.

Beattie, M., **Co-Dependent No More,** Center City, Minnesota: Hazelden Educational Materials, 1987.

Black, C., **It Will Never Happen To Me,** Denver: Medical Administration, 1982.

Covington, S., **Leaving the Enchanted Forest,** New York: Harper and Row, 1988.

Cork, M., **The Forgotten Children,** Toronto: Alcohol and Drug Addiction Research Foundation, 1969.

Dowling, C., **The Cinderella Complex: Women's Hidden Fear of Independence,** New York: Pocket Books, 1981.

Dyer, W. W., **Your Erroneous Zones,** New York: Funk and Wagnalls, 1976.

Elkin, M., **Families Under The Influence: Changing Alcoholic Patterns,** New York: W. W. Norton, 1984.

Forward, S., **Men Who Hate Women and the Women Who Love Them,** New York: Bantam Books, 1986.

Haley, Jay, **Uncommon Therapy: The Psychiatric Techniques of Milton H. Erickson, M.D.,** New York: W.W. Norton, 1973.

Kopp, S. B., **If You Meet The Buddha On The Road, Kill Him!,** New York: Bantam Books, 1981.

Kübler-Ross, E., **On Death And Dying,** New York: MacMillan Publishing, 1969.

Larsen, E., **Stage II Recovery: Life Beyond Addiction,** San Francisco: Harper and Row, 1985.

Lerner, R., **Daily Affirmations: For Adult Children of Alcoholics,** Pompano Beach, Florida: Health Communications, 1985.

Meehan, Bob, **Beyond the Yellow Brick Road: Our Children and Drugs,** New York: Contemporary Books, 1984.

Norwood, R., **Women Who Love Too Much,** Los Angeles: Jeremy P. Tarcher, 1985.

Powell, J., **Why Am I Afraid To Tell You Who I Am?** Niles, Illinois: Argus Communications, 1969.

Rubin, T., **The Angry Book,** New York: Macmillan, 1970.

Steiner, C., **Scripts People Live,** New York: Grove Press, 1979.

The 12 Steps For Adult Children, San Diego: Recovery Publications, 1987.

Wegschieder, S., **Another Chance: Hope and Health For The Alcoholic Family,** Palo Alto: Science and Behavior Books, 1981.

Whitfield, C. L., **Healing The Child Within,** Pompano Beach, Florida: Health Communications, 1987.

Woititz, J. G., **Adult Children of Alcoholics,** Pompano Beach, Florida: Health Communications, 1983.

BIBLIOGRAPHY

Ackerman, Robert J., **Children of Alcoholics: A Guide Book for Educators, Therapists, and Parents,** Holmes Beach, Florida: Learning Publications, 1983.

Ackerman, Robert J., **Let Go And Grow: Recovery For Adult Children of Alcoholics,** Pompano Beach, Florida: Health Communications, 1987.

Ackerman, Robert J., **Same House, Different Homes,** Pompano Beach, Florida: Health Communications, 1987.

Alcoholics Anonymous, **Twelve Steps and Twelve Traditions,** A.A. World Services, New York, 1952.

Beattie, Melody, "Co-Dependent No More," handout sheet, lecture, St. John's Health Center, St. Louis, Missouri, August 12, 1988.

Beattie, Melody, **Co-Dependent No More,** Center City, Minnesota, Hazelden Foundation, 1987.

Belson, Abby Avin, "Brain May Explain Why Some People Can't Have Fun," *New York Times,* 1983.

Black, Claudia, **It Will Never Happen To Me,** New York: Ballantine Books, 1981.

Black, Claudia, "Parental Alcoholism Leaves Most Kids Without Information, Feelings, Hope," *The Phoenix,* Volume 4, No. 11, November 1984.

Braiker, Harriet B., "Are You a Type E Woman?", *St. Louis Post-Dispatch,* March 22, 1987.

Cermak, Timmen L., **Diagnosing and Treating Co-dependence,** Minneapolis, Minnesota: Johnson Institute Books, 1986.

Cork, Margaret R., **The Forgotten Children,** Toronto: Addiction Research Foundation, 1969.

Dowling, Colette, **The Cinderella Complex — Women's Hidden Fears of Independence,** New York: Pocket Books, 1981.

Dyer, Wayne W., **Your Erroneous Zones,** New York: Funk and Wagnalls, 1976.

Forward, Susan, **Men Who Hate Women, and the Women Who Love Them,** New York: Bantam, 1986.

Friel, John; Subby, Robert, and Friel, Linda, **Co-Dependence And The Search For Identity,** Pompano Beach, Florida: Health Communications, 1984.

Gravitz, Herbert L., and Bowden, Julie D., **Recovery: A Guide For Adult Children of Alcoholics,** New York: Simon and Schuster, 1985.

Halpern, Howard, **How To Break Your Addiction To A Person,** New York: Bantam, 1983.

Johnson, Vernon E., **I'll Quit Tomorrow,** New York: Harper and Row, 1973.

Kopp, Sheldon B., **If You Meet the Buddha on the Road, Kill Him!,** New York: Bantam Books, 1972.

Kübler-Ross, Elisabeth, **On Death and Dying,** New York: MacMillan Publishing, 1969.

Larson, Earnie, **Stage II Recovery: Life Beyond Addiction,** San Francisco: Harper and Row, 1985.

Leerhson, Charles, and Namuth, Tessa, "Alcohol and the Family," *Newsweek,* January 18, 1988, page 62.

Lerner, Rokelle, **Daily Affirmations: For Adult Children Of Alcoholics,** Pompano Beach, Florida: Health Communications, 1985.

Lerner, Rokelle, "Young Children of Alcoholics," lecture presented at Seventh Annual Fall Conference on Alcoholism," Virginia Beach, Virginia, October 28-30, 1987.

Norwood, Robin, **Women Who Love Too Much,** Los Angeles: Jeremy P. Tarcher, 1985.

Phelps, Janice K., and Nourse, Alan E., **The Hidden Addictions and How To Get Free,** Boston: Little, Brown, 1986.

Powell, John, S.J., **Why Am I Afraid To Tell You Who I Am?,** Allen, Texas: Argus Communications, 1969.

Rubin, Theodore, **The Angry Book,** New York: MacMillan, 1970.

Seliger, Susan, "Making Stress Work For You," *McCall's,* June 1984, pages 125-131.

Shneideman, Edwin, "At the Point of No Return," *Psychology Today,* March 1987, pages 55-58.

Steiner, Claude M., **Scripts People Live,** New York: Grove Press, 1974.

Subby, Robert, **Lost In The Shuffle: The Co-dependent Reality,** Pompano Beach, Florida: Health Communications, 1987.

Unpublished, "Laundry List," New York City Adult Children of Alcoholics Al-Anon Group.

Wallace, John, **Alcoholism: New Light on the Disease,** Newport, Rhode Island: Edgehill Publications, 1985.

Wegscheider, Sharon, **Another Chance: Hope and Health for the Alcoholic Family,** Palo Alto: Science and Behavior Books, 1981.

Wegscheider-Cruse, Sharon, **Choicemaking,** Pompano Beach, Florida: Health Communications, 1985.

Wegscheider-Cruse, Sharon, "Co-dependency Treatment," lecture presented at Seventh Annual Fall Conference on Alcoholism, Virginia Beach, October 28-30, 1987.

Woititz, Janet Geringer, "Adult Children of Alcoholics," lecture presented at Seventh Annual Fall Conference on Alcoholism, Virginia Beach, October 28-30, 1987.

Woititz, Janet Geringer, **Adult Children Of Alcoholics,** Hollywood, Florida: Health Communications, 1983.